S0-ANN-611

Virtual Apprentice

FASHION DESIGNER

By Don Rauf
and Monique Vescia

Ferguson
An imprint of Infobase Publishing

Virtual Apprentice: Fashion Designer

Ferguson
An imprint of Infobase Publishing
132 West 31st Street
New York, NY 10001

Library of Congress Cataloging-in-Publication Data

Rauf, Don.
Virtual apprentice : fashion designer / Don Rauf and Monique Vescia.
p. cm.
Includes bibliographical references and index.
ISBN-13: 978-0-8160-6761-9
ISBN-10: 0-8160-6761-9
1. Fashion–History. 2. Fashion designers–History. I. Vescia, Monique. II. Title.
TT507.R29 2007
746.9'2–dc22
2007019426

Ferguson books are available at special discounts when purchased in bulk quantities for businesses, associations, institutions, or sales promotions. Please call our Special Sales Department in New York at (212) 967-8800 or (800) 322-8755.

You can find Ferguson on the World Wide Web at http://www.fergpubco.com

Produced by Bright Futures Press (http://www.brightfuturespress.com)
Series created by Diane Lindsey Reeves
Interior design by Tom Carling, carlingdesign.com
Cover design by Salvatore Luongo

Photo List: Table of Contents Rick Barrentine/Corbis; Page 5 Stu Collier/Dreamstime.com; Page 7 John Rawlings/Conde Nest Archives/ Corbis; Page 10 Hulton-Deutsch Collection/Corbis; Page 13 Iofoto/Dreamstime.com; Page 17 Rick Barrentine/Corbis; Page 19 Dwights/ Dreamstime.com; Page 20 Jjrmcv/Dreamstime.com; Page 25 Danish Khan; Page 27 Mitrofanova/Dreamstime.com; Page 31 Jjrmcv/Dreamstime.com; Page 32 Poppy Berry/Corbis; Page 35 Andreea Angelescu/Corbis; Chuck Savage/Corbis; Page 39 Lynn Goldsmith/Corbis.

Note to Readers: Please note that every effort was made to include accurate Web site addresses for kid-friendly resources listed throughout this book. However, Web site content and addresses change often and the author and publisher of this book cannot be held accountable for any inappropriate material that may appear on these Web sites. In the interest of keeping your online exploration safe and appropriate, we strongly suggest that all Internet searches be conducted under the supervision of a parent or other trusted adult.

Printed in the United States of America

BANG BFP 10 9 8 7 6 5 4 3 2 1

This book is printed on acid-free paper.

CONTENTS

INTRODUCTION

Welcome to the World of the Fashion Designer

Some people just seem to naturally have a gift for style and an eye for fashion. Maybe it's the girl in your homeroom who was the first to wear handmade, jeweled flip-flops. Maybe it's that uncle of yours whose colorful shirts are the talk of every family reunion. Or maybe it's you who jumpstarts the fashion trends at your school. Always the best-dressed one in the room, that person can walk into any closet and throw together an unexpected combination of garments and accessories that look amazing together. A few of these trendsetters even turn out to be famous fashion designers.

The world of fashion design is, in reality, a fiercely competitive profession with very little room at the top (picture a big, old pyramid) for anyone but the most mind-blowingly talented designers who combine artistry with hardheaded business sense. Still want to climb this glass pyramid? Suit yourself! Truly talented designers often do not see their career path as a choice; many are unfazed by the difficulties they face getting to the top because they have always believed that fashion, whatever else it may be, is their life

Virtual Apprentice: Fashion Designer lets you experience, firsthand what it's like to work in this creative, challenging, and competitive profession. Find out how a design concept moves from the fertile brain of the designer onto the runways at Fashion Week and finally onto the racks at Bloomingdale's. Travel from the haute couture fitting rooms of Paris to the funky fashions on the street, and along the way you'll learn about the latest trends and exciting new technologies in this field. Hear about fashion icons and fashion emergencies, and find out if you've got the goods (and how to get them) that you'll need to be on the cutting edge of this fabulous career.

Fashion looks to the future but draws upon the past for inspiration. So we've reserved you a front-row seat under the tents for a whirlwind tour of the history of fashion design.

Are your fashion designs destined for the runways of New York and Paris?

CHAPTER 1

The Evolution of Fashion

Scientists were able to figure out when humans first started to wear clothes with the help of a bug—the human body louse. This little parasite feeds on its human host and lays its eggs in clothing, so scientists speculate that clothes date back about 40,000 years, when these bugs first evolved.

Fashion functions as a means of social communication, a way of telling other people something important about you: what your job is (as the old song goes, "I see by your outfit that you are a cowboy"), how rich you are, whether you're married or single, gay or straight, and what your interests are. As British designer Katharine Hamnett says, "Clothes create a wordless means of communication that we all understand." Whether you're aware of it or not, you constantly judge other people by what they're wearing; you "size them up": Cool or uncool? Nerd or jock? Trendy or Goth? What you wear is influenced by your own tastes but also by where you live and go to school, your age, your religious beliefs, and many other factors.

Early humans began making and wearing clothing for a very practical reason: They were cold! But fashion today is both an elaborate system of communication and an art form that developed as human cultures evolved and grew more sophisticated.

During the Elizabethan Age (1558–1603), when Queen Elizabeth I was on the British throne, regulations called Sumptuary Laws provided strict guidelines for what people could

> "Clothes create a wordless means of communication that we all understand."
>
> —Katharine Hamnett, designer

and could not wear. Individuals belonging to the lower classes were not allowed to wear certain colors such as purple, crimson (a rich red), deep black, and pure white, because the dyes used to create them were very expensive. Working people could wear yellow, green, or pink garments, but never gold or silver. Only members of royalty could wear clothing trimmed with ermine fur. Punishments for violating these laws could be harsh: You might be put to death for wearing the wrong clothing–talk about a fashion victim!

How does this mid-twentieth-century fashion magazine cover compare to those you find on newstands today?

Do It Yourself

When you need a new pair of pants, you just drag your mom or dad to the mall and flip through the racks until you find a pair you like. But before the 1850s, people either made their own clothing or paid a seamstress or tailor to make them. And remember, people wore more undergarments in those days, which also had to be handmade. Before crinoline or hoop skirts were invented in 1856, a woman might wear six different petticoats under her dress to give it the proper fullness.

A Stitch in Time

"Fashion designer" is a relatively recent job description that did not even exist before 1858. Fashion design is closely related to the development of the garment industry or "rag trade" and the mechanical inventions that made that industry possible. In 1846 Elias Howe patented the first sewing machine. Howe's machine was powered by a hand crank, which meant that the operator had to stop work at intervals to crank it up. Isaac Singer improved upon Howe's design when he devised, in the 1850s, a machine powered with a foot treadle, leaving the worker's hands free to feed the fabric toward the mechanized needle as it moved up and down. Thanks to this laborsaving device, a shirt that might have taken 14 hours to sew by hand could be made in less than an hour and a half.

Before 1850, 70 percent of clothes worn were hand-sewn by the people who wore them.

Around this time a dressmaker named Ellen Demorest invented tissue-paper patterns. Customers who bought Madame Demorest's patterns could reproduce at home the same fashionable designs they admired in illustrated fashion magazines. (If you've done any sewing, you know that paper patterns are still used today.) Soon after, clothing sizes became standardized for the first time. All these improvements made it possible to produce factory-made garments in different sizes that people could purchase at a store or through a catalog. Now, rather than having to construct your own clothes or hire someone to make them for you, you could flip through the Sears Roebuck catalog, find a garment you liked, and order one in your size. People who lived

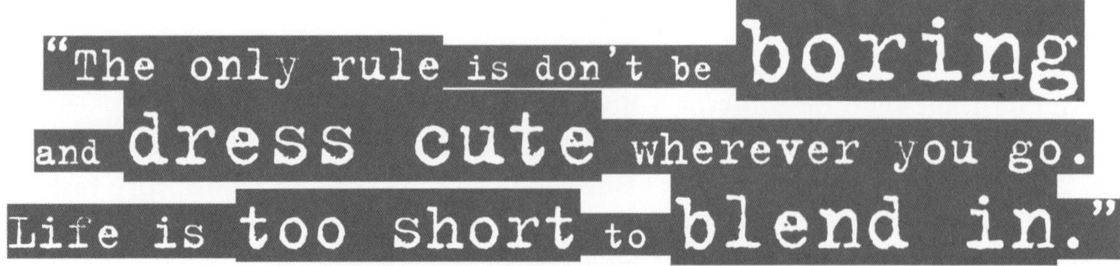

—PARIS HILTON, HOTEL HEIRESS

out in the country could dress in the same styles and fashions that their city cousins were wearing.

The most successful fashion designers were those who responded to or anticipated the changing times. During World War I (1914–1918), many women went to work in weapons factories and other industries. They needed clothing that was comfortable, functional, and suited to their new lifestyles and responsibilities. Women, who finally won the right to vote in 1922, wanted clothing that expressed their new freedoms and rights as citizens.

Tight Squeeze

Corsets were worn by men, women, and even children at different times throughout history. These uncomfortable undergarments were often stiffened with wires and whale baleen and featured hooks and laces that could be tightened to squeeze the waist down to a fashionably smaller size. But good luck taking a deep breath!

The House of Worth

The first real fashion designer was Charles Frederick Worth (1826–1895), "the father of haute couture," who established the House of Worth in 1858. Worth was born in England but moved to Paris when he was 19. He decided to open his own couture house when dresses he had designed for his fiancée attracted attention among upper-class women. Worth made dresses for royalty, such as the Empress Eugénie, wife of Napoleon III, as well as for the Rothschilds and the Vanderbilts–the 19th-century equivalents of today's Trump or Hilton families. Worth was the first person to sew his own label into the garments that he designed. Worth also invented the fashion show, since before that designs were shown on dolls (these might be small or life-sized) rather than on live models.

Paris, the Capital of Style

In the early 20th century, Paris was the fashion capital of the world. Another important French designer from this time was Paul Poiret (1879–1944), an apprentice of Worth. Poiret favored a long, straight silhouette with no corset underneath. He also introduced the "hobble skirt," which was full at the hips and extremely narrow at the ankles, requiring women to walk with tiny steps. Discussing his designs, Poiret declared, "I freed the bust but I shackled the legs."

Madame Jeanne Paquin (1869–1936) was the first woman to become a leading fashion designer. She opened her own *maison de couture* in 1890 next to the House of Worth. In the 1920s a French designer named Madeleine Vionnet introduced the "bias cut": the practice of cutting diagonally across the weave of the fabric. This makes the material cling to the body. As a result of Vionnet's innovation, certain styles of that period were very slender and form-fitting.

Chanel: A Paris Original

The French fashion scene produced one of the most influential and original designers of all time: Gabrielle "Coco" Chanel (1883–1971). Chanel began as a hat designer and then turned her talents to apparel. Her strategy was to borrow styles, fabrics, and articles of clothing from menswear and to adapt these for women. Chanel once observed that "Fashion is architecture: it is a matter of proportions," and the proportions she favored were long and lean. Her trademark look, in the 1920s and 1930s, was an easy-to-wear women's suit that became a wardrobe classic. Chanel's designs have inspired countless "knock-offs," or cheap imitations, a practice that Chanel actually encouraged: "I want my dresses to go out on the street," she declared. Chanel introduced the "little black dress" as well as the first perfume to bear a designer's name: Chanel No. 5. This timeless couturier was still working on a collection when she died at age 87; oddly enough, at the time of her death she had a Paris wardrobe consisting of just three outfits.

Although Coco Chanel's fashion designs became famous in the early 1900s, they are still considered classics today.

Great designers like Chanel establish design empires, or fashion houses, and then pass their unique vision on to the designers that follow in their fashionable footsteps. The current head designer at the House of Chanel, Karl Lagerfeld, must

"Fashion is architecture: it is a matter of proportions."
—COCO CHANEL

maintain the classic Chanel brand while making sure the company's designs are stylish and up-to-date.

International Influences

Most countries around the world have their own fashion industries, but only five have won international recognition: France, the United Kingdom, the United States, Italy, and Japan. In addition to Chanel, another important French designer was Christian Dior, who introduced a style in 1947 that came to be called "the New Look." Dior's tiny-waisted dresses with full skirts weren't really a new style at all, but they became very popular. During the 1960s, British designers such as Mary Quant and Vivienne Westwood put "Swinging London" on the fashion map with a youthful look that featured miniskirts and ankle boots as well as geometric shapes and wildly colorful prints. Today, Alexander McQueen, Hussein Chalayan, and John Galliano are among the most influential British designers. Some of the best-known American designers include Calvin Klein, Ralph Lauren, Anna Sui, and Donna Karan, the designer behind the DKNY label. Top-tier Italian designers include Valentino, Giorgio Armani, and Prada. The first Japanese designer to achieve international recognition was Hanae Mori, who artfully blended Eastern and Western influences in her styles. Other important Japanese designers include Issey Miyake and Rei Kawakubo, the designing woman behind the Comme des Garcons label.

The Height of Fashion

Haute couture (pronounced oat-cooTOUR) is French for "high sewing" and represents the highest expression of fashion as an art form. Haute couture is the finest clothing sewed by hand to the exact measurements of the wealthiest clientele. A haute couture garment is custom-made and requires an average of three fittings with the client. An evening gown with embroidery might require several thousand hours of work. Owning such a garment might cost anywhere from $26,000 to $100,000–but you'll never have to show up at a party and see someone else wearing the same dress!

To earn the distinction of a "haute couture" label, a designer must belong to the *Chambre Syndicale de la Haute Couture*, an organization founded in 1868 by Charles Frederick Worth and his sons to prevent couture designs from being copied. Today, members of this incredibly elite group include designers Chanel, Christian Dior, Hubert de Givenchy, Christian Lacroix, Jean Paul Gaultier, and Hanae Mori, among others.

CHECK IT OUT

Visit http://www.hel-looks.com to check out what fab and funky fashions people are wearing on the streets of Helsinki, the capital of Finland.

Sources of Style

Besides haute couture, there are two main categories of fashion design: ready to wear and mass market. Designs in ready-to-wear collections are presented during Fashion Week in fashion capitals such as New York City; Milan, Italy; and Madrid, Spain. Ready-to-wear designs are produced in limited numbers from high-quality fabrics. These styles influence the mass-market category, which consists of clothing produced quickly and cheaply: your Gap cargo pants, for instance. Fashion for the masses trickles down from what shows on the runways. An exaggerated feature, such as one season's multiple layering pieces, may show up in a scaled-down version (layered T-shirts, perhaps) on the headless mannequins at Kohl's.

But "the street" is also an important source of fashion trends. Since the late 1960s, the latest new styles and trends have tended to bubble up from looks first seen on the street–fashions teens invent and adopt that express the mood, tastes, and interests of youth culture. You and your friends have an influence on what types of fashions appear on the runways next season, and industry trend watchers pay close attention. (Whoa, check out the camo spats and silver mini-poncho on that guy!)

Movie Stars and the Mass Market

Movies are seen by millions of people, and over the years Hollywood has exerted a powerful influence over fashion. Blue jeans,

Photo shoots are a glamorous part of the fashion world.

the article of clothing most associated with American culture (we challenge you to find someone who doesn't own at least one pair), were considered just work clothes until James Dean wore them in *Rebel Without a Cause* (1955). Back in the 1970s, Diane Keaton's character in the Woody Allen film *Annie Hall* (1977) spurred a generation of young women to copy her kooky take on menswear. Madonna's punk-inspired miniskirts, torn fishnets, lacy gloves, and underwear worn as outerwear–featured in her

"A designer is only as good as the star who wears her clothes."
—COSTUME DESIGNER EDITH HEAD

music videos and the film *Desperately Seeking Susan*—inspired many imitators during the 1980s. The accessories business gets a big boost from Hollywood, too. The hip look of stars Will Smith and Tommy Lee Jones in the 1997 movie *Men in Black* made Ray-Ban sunglasses hip again. Costume designer Edith Head, who won eight Academy Awards for her fashions, once said that "A designer is only as good as the star who wears her clothes." And the star who had the greatest impact on fashion design was the actress Audrey Hepburn (1929–1993). With her willowy silhouette and dancer's posture, her natural style and elegance, Hepburn was the perfect person to showcase the fashions of French designer Hubert de Givenchy. No other actress before or since has had such a profound and long-lasting influence on fashion.

FIND OUT MORE

Hubert de Givenchy designed the clothing for many of Audrey Hepburn's films, including *Funny Face* (1957), *Love in the Afternoon* (1957), *Breakfast at Tiffany's* (1961), and *Charade* (1964). Rent one of these films and you'll see why Hepburn became an unforgettable fashion icon.

Rockin' the Runway

Since Elvis hit the music charts in 1956 and appeared on *The Ed Sullivan Show* before a TV audience of 60 million viewers, the performances of pop stars and rock musicians have also driven fashion trends. The beehive hairdos and shimmery dresses of Diana Ross and the Supremes, the Beatles' ankle boots and haircuts, Jimi Hendrix's psychedelic style, and David Bowie's space-fantasy mix of male and female were all seen and imitated by countless fans.

More recently, hip-hop music has had the greatest impact on fashion. Labels such as Phat Farm, Tommy Hilfiger, and FUBU have turned hip-hop's urban street style into a massive business. The rapper and music producer Sean "P. Diddy" Combs, always known as a snappy dresser, launched a very successful line of sportswear in 1998 under the Sean John brand. Combs's fashion empire has since branched out to include more upscale men's suits and women's wear, once again getting a warm welcome from fashion buyers. In 2004, Combs was named CFDA Menswear Designer of the Year (that's the Oscar of fashion), beating out Ralph Lauren and Michael Kors.

Fashion Forward

Every fashion designer needs to know about the history of fashion since styles and silhouettes from the past are constantly being recycled with a brand-new spin. (Just when we thought we were safe, here come those leg warmers again!) Finally, every successful designer knows that the fashion industry is fueled not by need (nobody "needs" a $2,000 handbag) but by desire. As American designer Ralph Lauren once said, "I don't design clothes, I design dreams."

CHAPTER 2

Fashion Designer at Work

You have slaved for months, working around the clock and even on weekends, all for this big moment. You are a young, independent fashion designer, and today you are presenting your latest line of clothing at an important runway show. Models are parading down the catwalk wearing your original designs. Camera flashes go off as the press reports on your new look. A few celebrities are even scattered in the audience–so many people love the world of fashion, and they're all excited to see your latest designs.

Most important, the audience is filled with fashion buyers from boutiques, specialty stores, and major department stores. At the end, you hope the applause you hear from the crowd will translate into sales, and you will have a popular line of clothing. At the celebration afterward you find out that many buyers have already placed orders for your designs, and you sit back and finally relax.

You put in so much hard work to reach this point. The life of a fashion designer is 100 times busier than you had ever dreamed. The show itself was over in 15 minutes, but many months of hard work and a ton of money went into getting it all together. A typical runway show costs about $100,000.

FUN FACTOID

French footwear designer Christian Louboutin found a way to make his designs instantly recognizable: Every pair of Louboutin shoes sports lipstick-red soles. How's that for a hot foot?

"Style is primarily a matter of instinct."

—AMERICAN DESIGNER BILL BLASS

You cut corners and were able to do it for just $20,000. Still, you had to hire the right models, a fashion stylist, a hair stylist, a makeup artist, and a couple of assistants to make sure your show was a knockout. You also needed to send out invitations, hire a

Fashion designers work in a colorful world of fabrics and ideas.

POP QUIZ

Accessory to a Fashion...Disaster?

Find out how well you can put together an outfit by matching the garments with the appropriate accessories.

1 A flippy flower-print skirt and a tank top

2 A three-piece seersucker suit

3 Cargo pants and a polo shirt

4 A floor-length bias-cut gown with spaghetti straps

5 Cropped jeans and an embroidered V-neck tunic

6 Flannel pajamas with rubber duckies all over them

A A Panama hat and a false mustache

B Fuzzy yellow slippers and a cup of warm milk

C A crocheted hoodie and jelly flip-flops

D A faux fur wrap and strappy silver high-heeled sandals

E Retro sneakers and wraparound sunglasses

F Bangle bracelets and espadrille shoes

ANSWERS: 1-C, 2-A, 3-E, 4-D, 5-F, 6-B

But those are just the most obvious match-ups. An adventurous designer is full of surprises and might make an evening-gown-and-fuzzy-slipper combo the next big thing!

publicist, and rent the right lighting. These preparations took just a fraction of your energy. Many months of your time went into making the 40 dresses that your models wore on the runway. And on top of designing, you devoted a lot of time to the business end of being a designer, from raising the cash to set up your workspace to paying your electricity bill.

Taking the Independent Route

Most clothes are created by unknown designers who work behind the scenes. They work for apparel manufacturers and crank out looks that will be mass-produced. Sometimes they don't originate the ideas but come up with slightly modified versions of popular trends. They typically design in small workspaces surrounded by the bustle of pattern makers and sample sewers. The pace can be grueling as they prepare fall, winter, spring, and summer collections.

As an independent designer, your work schedule may be even busier. You're following a different path, building your own label. You're setting out to establish yourself as a name that means fashion–like Calvin Klein, Vera Wang, Giorgio Armani, and Donna Karan.

Long before the runway show, your design process began inside your head. You had to think of an original look for your clothing that people would buy. Then, using ink and pencil and sometimes pastel crayons, color pencils, or watercolor paints, you put your ideas on paper. You visualized the shapes, cuts, colors, and patterns and created sketches to help communicate your design ideas to others.

You work in an airy, well-lit workspace. A big work table room gives you a place to stretch out your fabric and space for a couple of sewing machines and large bolts of fabric. You also have clothes racks holding your in-progress designs as well as finished

Fashionistas find the latest looks in boutiques like this one.

The latest fashion trends get their start on a designer's sketchpad.

products. A few headless dressmaker's forms stand by ready to help–you drape fabric on them during the beginning, construction phase of your clothes. While most of your space is devoted to hands-on design work, you also have a small area dedicated to the business end–a desk, computer, and files to manage bills, place orders, and track the paperwork.

First Inspiration, Then Perspiration

As an up-and-coming designer, you are certainly up early and coming along with your design plans, pushing them forward every day. To make it in this business, you have to eat, sleep, and breathe fashion. Every moment before your runway show was especially focused on your creations.

Your inspiration for your clothes comes from your concern for the environment. Your eco-friendly designs include cottons that were not sprayed with pesticide and yarns made from organically grown bamboo. You only buy fabric from companies that support fair labor practices. Your designs, while they are rich with earth tones–deep clay reds and muted browns–are also fun yet classy evening wear. It's a unique combination that sets you apart. You want to show that "greens" can have a good time while making the world a better place.

A Frantic Day in Fashion

Flashback to a month before your big runway show. You begin this day like most others–long before dawn with a strong cup of coffee and a stack of the latest magazines about pop culture and fashion. You feel more confident about your collection as you flip through the magazines and notice more people talking about climate change. The latest movies, music, and books show a growing interest in saving the planet. (When you sketched out your designs a year ago, you thought you had a hunch that you were on the cutting-edge of a growing trend. You always try to keep up with what's hot and what's not.) You tear out a few pages that catch your interest–they may give you new ideas for future designs.

Before 8 a.m., you review your e-mails and catch up on paperwork. You pay the bills and review orders for your previous clothing collection. You place a call to a manufacturer in Hong Kong to make sure they are on schedule. You were lucky to have a major department store agree to sell some of your fashions, so you found a company that could manufacture a large number of your garments for a reasonable price. You toured the plant in Hong Kong about a year ago to make sure that work conditions there were good for the employees. When your big fashion show is over, you've scheduled a trip abroad to visit the manufacturer. You also want to

Field Trip to a Fabric Store

FIND OUT MORE

To get inspired, go to a fabric or craft store and look at all the different materials on display. Use your eyes AND your hands to browse through the selections (feeling the texture and weight of the fabric). Then page through a few pattern books, paying special attention to the designers' collections. Pattern envelopes feature a lot of important information on the back, such as level of technical difficulty, which materials are best suited for the pattern, and how much yardage (yards of fabric) is needed for each size. While you're there, you can pick up some material to play with at home. "Remnants"—pieces of leftover fabric at the ends of rolls or "bolts" of material—are always available at a discount. Start your own swatch collection by purchasing small pieces of some of your favorites.

tour factories in Taiwan and Korea. Then you'll continue on to France and Italy where you'll visit boutiques and shop for fabrics. While you're thinking of fabrics, you take stock of the bolts of fabric you have in your studio. You want to make sure you have enough on hand to finish your outfits. You also check sales reports from the various retailers that sell your clothes–you want to get a sense of what's moving (off the racks, that is) and what is not.

At nine o'clock, your two assistants arrive, and it's right down to work. They help you cut patterns, drape fabric on the dress forms, and stitch together your designs. It's only the three of you, but the room is buzzing with activity: scissors flashing, measuring tape unraveling, thick chalk marking the fabric, the sewing machine needle flying up and down through the fabric. You are making up sample garments called *toiles*, constructed of a plain-colored material called muslin. You don't want to waste expensive fabric on a design that is not working, so you always make up a toile first to check the fit.

At 10:30 a.m. you meet with your assistants to see how the work is coming along. One of your helpers is experienced at CAD (computer-aided design), and he has created a virtual model onscreen. The model is wearing one of your designs. You compare the real outfit being put together in the room to the one worn by the virtual model on the computer. (You joke that the virtual model looks like she's gained some weight!)

After lunch, the real models are coming in to your studio to be fitted for your show. The right model can make all the difference in making a design look fantastic on the runway, and that can add up to more sales. When the models come in, you take detailed measurements and have them try on the clothes that are nearing

Factory Fire

FIND OUT MORE

On March 25, 1911, a fire broke out in the Triangle Shirtwaist Factory in New York City. Young female workers, most of them immigrants, were unable to escape because the doors were kept locked by the factory owners to prevent employees from leaving. Many burned to death or jumped to escape the flames, and 146 workers perished in the fire. This disaster helped make the public aware of the terrible working conditions in the garment industry. You can see the plaques commemorating this tragedy on the building where the fire occurred, on the corner of Washington Place and Green Street, now part of New York University, or go to http://www.ilr.cornell.edu/trianglefire/ to learn more about what happened.

completion. You want all the clothing to fit perfectly. To make it in this business, perfection is key.

Later that day you have a meeting with your hair stylist and makeup artist. The looks they create with your models will be part of a complete vision you send down the runway. The hair and makeup on the models have to complement the overall look of your collection.

At the very end of the day you meet with your Web designer. She helps you maintain a site where you can display and sell your clothes online. After dinner, your day is not over. You're going to meet friends at an art gallery and then head from there to a rock concert. Sure, it will be fun, but it's also part of your job. You'll take careful note of what the artists, gallery visitors, musicians, and concert goers are wearing. Trends often start with those involved in the arts. If you see anything that strikes you, you'll whip out a little sketchpad that you always carry with you. You never know where inspiration will come from. Anything from the green, aging copper of a city rooftop to the graffiti on a wall can trigger ideas for your next fashion masterpiece. In fact, as you return to your apartment for the night, the doorman's uniform gives you an idea. Before bed, you roughly sketch some of your concepts. You can already picture your hit runway show for next season.

Transform a T-shirt

Take the Virtual Apprentice T-shirt Challenge: Find an old T-shirt. See how long it takes you to cut, tear, stitch, staple, glue, paint, or otherwise alter that shirt into a work of wearable art. Now here's the real challenge: Have you succeeded in producing a garment that you'd actually be proud to wear? If you can't wait to show off your latest creation, you may have some potential to become the next big name in fashion (with lots more training and experience, of course!).

CHAPTER 3

Fashion Design Tech and Trends

FIND OUT MORE

Corsets that constrict breathing, crinolines that catch fire...Do women still risk life and limb just to be fashionable? Some suggest that today the corset has simply become internalized in the form of diets, exercise, and cosmetic surgery. What do you think? Browse through the latest issues of fashion magazines like *ELLEgirl*, *Glamour*, *Allure*, and *Teen Vogue* to see if any of the styles look fatally attractive.

More than any other profession, fashion design is driven by trends. So no matter how cool you think you look today, the time will come when you'll think back on what you're wearing and shudder with utter embarrassment. That's what keeps the fashion biz going. As Coco Chanel once observed, "Fashion is made to become unfashionable." Here are some of today's latest trends and newest technologies in fashion design, but, beware, they'll probably be out of fashion tomorrow!

Taking the Runway on the Road

Until recently, important runway shows have been held in fashion capitals such as New York and Paris for a specialized audience of industry insiders and celebrities. But some promoters got the bright idea of feeding the public's growing interest in high fashion by putting these shows on the road and bringing them to cities such as Houston and Chicago. Ticket prices range from $500 to $1,500–would YOU pay that much for a runway seat?

> "Fashions fade, style is eternal."
>
> –FRENCH DESIGNER YVES SAINT LAURENT

High-Tech, High Fashion

One of the most useful new technologies in fashion design is known as CAD, which stands for computer-aided design. New software enables designers to transfer paper ("hard") patterns into digital (or "soft") form on the computer using a digitizer or puck (like a mouse) or a stylus (like a pen). 3-D design modules let you preview a design on a virtual model to check fit and see how the fabric behaves. Some CAD systems include animation so you can see the model in action. This reduces the trouble and expense of actually creating a sample garment. Designers can

Fashionable fabrics are made from fibers in factories like this.

also send patterns quickly to manufacturers via electronic files. CAD systems are pricey (thousands of dollars) and out of the range of most individual designers, but they can save large design firms lots of time and money.

Men in Skirts

While the Scottish tradition of kilts may date back as early as 375 A.D. and men in Southeast Asia regularly wear sarongs, American men have been far more reluctant to give up pants in favor of skirts. But a store in Seattle, Washington, called Utilikilts is trying to change that, one pair of hairy knees at a time. Utilikilts sells lots of kilts each year to men confident enough to be seen in a skirt. But being this fashion forward comes at a price–Utilikilts start at around $130 bucks.

CHECK IT OUT: The Shelf Life of a Style

James Laver, a noted British costume historian, created this timeline of style called "Laver's Law":

- Indecent—10 years before its time
- Shameless—5 years before its time
- Daring—1 year before its time
- Smart---------------
- Dowdy—1 year after its time
- Hideous—10 years after its time
- Ridiculous—20 years after its time
- Amusing—30 years after its time
- Quaint—50 years after its time
- Charming—70 years after its time
- Romantic—100 years after its time
- Beautiful—150 years after its time

No More Sweatshops

Since the earliest days of the industry, garment workers (often children and women) have suffered poor and unhealthy work conditions, long hours, and low pay. Advocacy groups such as the Clean Clothes Campaign (http://www.cleanclothes.org) are raising consumer awareness about this issue by asking people to buy "sweatfree" clothing from companies that do not treat workers unfairly.

Weighty Matters

After 14-year-old Brazilian model Maiara Galvao Vieira died from complications related to the eating disorder anorexia nervosa, the organizers of Madrid Fashion Week made headlines in 2006 when they barred too-skinny models from participating in runway shows. Soon after, the Italian Chamber of Fashion decreed that models who walk the Milan runways must have a license that proves they are at least 16 years old and in good health.

Geek Fashions?

Technology, science, and fashion have converged, with some amazing results, in so-called smart fabrics. Jackets with built-in MP3 players and headphones, tank tops woven of optical fibers that glow in the dark, and T-shirts with embedded TV screens wowed audiences at fashion shows held at MIT (the Massachusetts Institute of Technology). "Wearables" are garment designs that incorporate the electronic devices that people usually carry with them such as cell phones and PDAs–leaving hands free to shop for even more stuff.

What colors are hot this season?

The Wearin' of the Green

It may look white and fluffy, but environmentalists call cotton the world's "dirtiest" crop. Growers use tons of pesticides to keep the bugs off their cotton. All these chemicals pollute the environment and harm the people who harvest the cotton. The eco-fashion movement encourages consumers to choose fabrics, such as organic cotton, hemp, and bamboo, that are easy on the earth. Pioneers of the eco-fashion movement include designers Linda Loudermilk and Katharine Hamnett, who uses 100 percent organic cotton in her menswear. Learn more about the price the world pays for cotton at http://www.ejfoundation.org/cotton.

Canine Couture

Your dog is your best friend–and now he can be your best man, in a custom-made doggie tuxedo! Elaborate dog clothes and footwear are all the rage, and dog lovers pay top dollar for canine jogging suits, PJs, and even bridal wear. Design firms that usually cater to humans are jumping on the gravy train: Check out Juicy

Couture's line of dog clothes and accessories at http://www.pawpalaceonline.com. Woof!

Design Diva

Rock and pop musicians have had a big influence on fashion trends. Now some of those stars hope to capitalize on their status as fashion icons by starting their own clothing lines. One of the most successful pop-star-turned-designers is Gwen Stefani, whose strong sense of style was always on display in performances with her band No Doubt. Stefani's L.A.M.B. line, launched in 2004, received a warm welcome on the runways. Stefani's second line, Harajuku Lovers, based on Japanese street fashion, was launched in 2005.

Just Your Average Guy

Male models on the runways have tended to fall into the hunk or the waif category, with not much in between. But a recent trend in men's fashion has been a preference for models that look less exotic and extreme and more like "regular" guys–or at least incredibly handsome and buff regular guys!

Are You a Leader or a Follower?

Do people constantly come up to you and ask where you got what you're wearing? Are you considered a trendsetter at your school, or do you play it safe and try to dress like the other kids you hang with? Well, here's a little secret: The people who set trends don't follow fashion. They have their own style and they stick to it. So if you want a future in fashion design, don't waste time trying to keep up with the trends—create your own instead.

Reality Design Shows

Now through five seasons, Bravo's *Project Runway*, the televised design competition hosted by supermodel Heidi Klum, continues to attract a faithful following of male and female viewers. During each episode, aspiring designers face a different fashion challenge, like having to construct a wearable garment entirely out of recyclable waste. Since the show first aired, fashion design schools have reported a big jump in the number of applications they receive annually. (Read our interview with *Project Runway* alum Alison Kelly.)

Fowl Weather Gear

Scientists are researching ways of turning chicken feathers into fabric. These chicken farm byproducts are abundant, biodegrad-

Fatal Fads

The practice of decorating hats with ostrich plumes first began 400 years ago. By the 1890s, women were wearing entire bodies of smaller birds on their hats and clothing. Until the early 20th century, corset makers used whale baleen to strengthen undergarments and almost wiped out the bowhead whale population. A fashion for leopard skin coats helped drive these animals to the brink of extinction. Some current designers, like Stella McCartney (daughter of former Beatle Paul) and *Project Runway* winner Jay McCarroll, take a stand by refusing to incorporate fur into their collections. What are the environmental consequences of your fashion choices?

able, and have to the potential to be transformed into a lightweight fabric that is warmer than wool. Can you picture yourself strutting around in a chicken feather sweater?

What Is the Invisible Man Wearing?

A professor of engineering in Tokyo, Japan, has invented a "see-through" coat designed to make the wearer actually look transparent. The technology, the brainchild of professor Susumu Tachi, is very sophisticated, but basically, viewfinders built into a luminous jacket are able to project images from in front and behind a person onto the garment itself. This amazing coat uses technology to create the illusion that you're looking right through the person wearing it!

Wear Your Heart on Your Sleeve

The Heart Truth show, part of the Red Dress project headed by first lady Laura Bush, is an annual event at New York Fashion Week dedicated to raising awareness about heart disease in women. Famous designers pair up with famous female celebrities who walk the runway in red fashions. The 2007 show featured the work of designers Carolina Herrera, Bill Blass, Gustavo Cadile, and others.

CHAPTER 4

Fashion Industry Sweat and Shears

If you see yourself as an artistic type, you can express yourself in many ways–in painting, in film, in music, in theater. Fashion designers are artists who express themselves in fabric. They have a vision of how people can be dressed. They have a sense of style and a blend of very distinct skills. But in this field you also need to be a businessperson. You have to have a sense of trends and what types of fashions sell. You have to be "crafty"–able to sew, take measurements, make patterns, cut fabric, and stitch it all together into outfits that make people say, "Where did you get that?"

To become a top designer, nothing beats hands-on experience. While you'll probably need to get professional training in college later on, you can start at an early age to weave together the knowledge and experience needed for this job.

FUN FACTOID

Designer Hussein Chalayan became infamous when, for his graduation show from the famous Central Saint Martins design school in London, he featured rotting clothes that he had buried in his backyard and then dug up for the show. For another show, Chalayan dressed his models in garments made from sugar glass that they smashed onstage with tiny hammers.

Is Fashion in Your Genes?

Often designers get bit by the fashion bug at a young age. Designer John Galliano was hooked on fashion as a boy when his mother would dress him in his "Sunday best." A first step toward becoming a fashion pro is taking an interest in your own clothes. As a future designer, you take pride in what you wear,

> "I base my fashion taste on what doesn't itch."
>
> —Gilda Radner, comedian

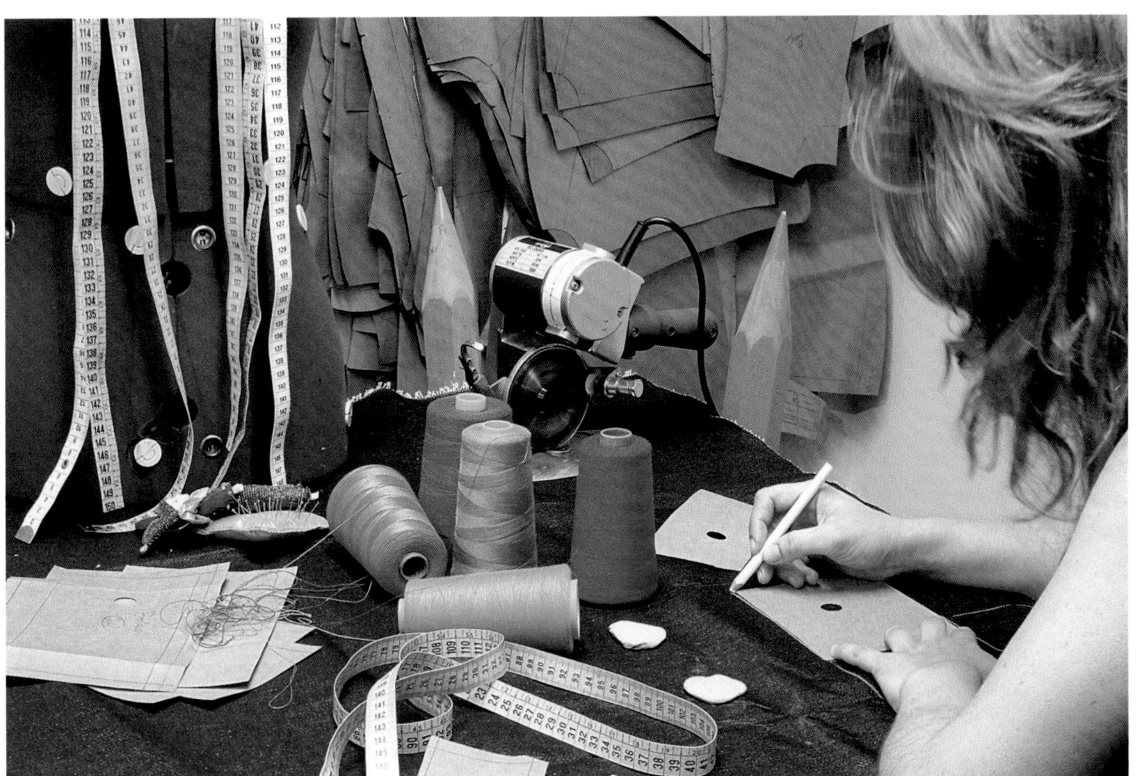

Learning how to sew is a good idea for future fashion designers.

and you have a sense of what looks good on you. You're aware of what people are wearing, but you're not afraid to dress in your own cool way. Designers are unique individuals, after all.

To know what's popular, you read entertainment magazines and follow the latest looks of actors and musicians, who often wear the most stylish "threads." You page through fashion magazines like *Vogue, Elle,* and *GQ,* and study how celebrities are dressing in *People, Us, Rolling Stone,* and other pop culture publications. You never miss TV shows dedicated to fashion such as *Project Runway, What Not to Wear,* and *America's Next Top Model.* When you see any movie or show, you pay close attention to the costumes, which were all dreamed up by professionals who have found their fashion niche in costume design. Halloween may be your favorite holiday, and you devote hours to preparing your costumes. When you go to museums and read history books, you take note of what people wore in times gone by. Although suits of armor will probably never be in style again, you can find inspiration in many styles from the past.

You enjoy your art classes. You have a keen sense of how colors work together. You appreciate patterns, textures, and shapes. As a future designer, you're already learning how to sketch because that's usually the first step in designing. You have to be able to get your ideas down on paper so others can visualize them. Renowned designer Jean-Paul Gaultier had no formal fashion training, but at a young age he started sending sketches to couture stylists. When established designer Pierre Cardin spot-

Aspiring fashion designers keep up with the latest fashions.

How Handy Are You?

Fashion designers bring their ideas to life by draping, cutting, and stitching together their creations. To determine if you've got "mad skills," grab a piece of paper and answer the following questions Yes or No.

A I can sew by hand and on a machine. (Y or N)

B I create handmade gifts for my friends and family. (Y or N)

C I know which colors are complementary and which ones clash. (Y or N)

D I love to give people fashion makeovers. (Y or N)

E I like to make my own clothes. (Y or N)

F I can sketch human figures. (Y or N)

G I can tell the difference between satin and silk. (Y or N)

If you answered yes to 5 out of 7 questions, you're a hands-on person who already possesses "starter" skills that will prove useful in fashion design. If you're all thumbs and you can't distinguish between robin's egg blue and periwinkle, you'll need to take some courses or find someone to help you learn the ropes.

ted Gaultier's talent, he hired him. Bill Blass loved drawing as a child, and at age 15 he began selling sketches of evening gowns for $25 each to a New York manufacturer.

When you're just starting out in fashion, most likely you will be a one-person apparel-making machine. You'll have to rely on your own talents to bring your designs to life. That's why you need hands-on clothes-crafting skills. You have to master basic skills, such as sewing by hand and with a machine, cutting fabric, following patterns, and making your own. A pattern is really the blueprint or instructions for how to construct a garment. It consists of pieces of paper shaped like the pieces of fabric that are to be sewn together. Designers learn how to sew the parts together and

Coming Apart at the Seams

FIND OUT MORE

You can learn a lot about how a garment is constructed by taking one apart. Find an old piece of clothing (something more complicated than a T-shirt, if possible) that's bound for the trash can and cut it apart along the seams. Spread the pieces flat on a table and study the shapes. How are curved shapes, such as sleeves and blouse fronts, created from flat fabric? How are collars constructed and attached to the garment? Can you reassemble the puzzle (using pins) after you've taken it apart?

fit them on a model. You can take on sewing as a hobby as soon as you can thread a needle. Designer Todd Oldham says he learned to sew at age nine from his mother and grandmother. Donna Karan picked up techniques from her father, who was a tailor. Learning to hem a skirt, make a pleat, or sew a seam at a young age is valuable experience. You can even start simply: Try tie-dying T-shirts to gain experience with fabric, color, and design. Or give your sneakers a makeover using a glue gun and beads or other decorations.

If you want to really hone your skills, you can sign up for a sewing or fashion design summer camp. You can find a list of camps at http://www.lovetosew.com. School clubs and youth organizations like 4-H often also offer classes in sewing and pattern making. Some schools even offer this training as part of family and consumer science education. Fabric and craft stores frequently offer sewing classes, too. Or you may know a friend or relative who sews and can lend you a machine and guide you through the process.

More than any other art form, fashion is tied to selling and commerce. Artists who paint or sculpt may not be thinking of a target audience that will buy their creations. But the goal of the fashion designer is to make clothes that people will buy. That's why the top designers are also great businesspeople. They are self-starters. They are entrepreneurs, which means they know how to begin their own businesses and run them successfully. If you've ever had a lemonade stand, sold comic books, washed cars, or mowed lawns for money, you have some experience running your own business.

Tommy Hilfiger was a born entrepreneur. At age 18 he would trek down to New York City from his hometown of Elmira in upstate New York to get his hands on jeans and bell-bottom pants. He then customized the pants and resold them at a store in his town. He went on to become one of the top menswear designers in the country and eventually sold his entire company for more than $1 billion.

So many talents come together in fashion. You have to be an excellent communicator to pitch your ideas and work with a team. You can build your communication skills by keeping up with your English courses. Math skills come in handy for the business side of fashion and for all the detailed measurements. Designers use problem-solving skills on a daily basis.

High school students can even get work experience that will give them a glimpse into the real world of fashion. When you're able to work a part-time or summer job, look into jobs at stores that sell clothing. By assisting in a clothing department at a major department store or selling in a boutique, you'll get a sense of what fashions are popular and how clothes are displayed and sold. Designer Ralph Lauren, who created the Polo line, worked part-time as a salesperson at Alexander's department store in New York. You might even find work helping a stylist, fashion photographer, or tailor.

Shows like Bravo TV's *Project Runway* provide opportunities for promising new designers.

College Couture

While some make it in the design world with sheer energy, smarts, and dedication, many head to a college with a focus on fashion. Fashion is a fast-paced, high-powered, big-money industry, so it pays to learn the latest about the business, textiles, fabrics, ornamentation, and fashion trends. New York's Fashion Institute of Technology and Parson's School of Design are famous for their fashion programs, but there are many other two-year and four-year schools offering this specific training.

College courses help students develop professional skills in sketching, pattern making, and sewing. While patterns are still made with pencil and paper (these are called *hard patterns*), some are now designed on computers (these are called *soft patterns*). College fashion students often master CAD, or computer-aided design systems, to create these patterns. Using computers, they may become virtual designers who fit their designs on virtual models on the computer screen.

Still, students need to understand how various garments fit real bodies and often study anatomy to help with this. As a student, you also learn the A to Z of clothing production. You'll spend time in fabric stores, surrounding yourself with big bolts of fabrics–from silk chemise to fake fur–the options are endless.

A lot of your time in school is devoted to developing your original style–a look that is uniquely your own. You are con-

POP QUIZ

How's Your Fashion Sense?

Grab a piece of paper and fill in the blanks to complete these sentences:

1 Very few customers can afford those exquisitely made garments known as haute couture, which is French for __________.

2 The __________ cut, invented in the 1920s by Madeleine Vionnet, inspired designers to create slinky gowns that clung close to the body.

3 During the design process, the couturier creates a sample called a __________ using an inexpensive fabric such as muslin.

4 The first designer to establish his own fashion house was named __________.

5 Besides haute couture, the two main categories of the fashion industry are __________ and __________.

6. The five nations with international reputations in fashion are France, the U.S., the U.K., Italy, and __________.

ANSWERS: 1-high sewing, 2-bias, 3-toile, 4-Charles Frederick Worth, 5-ready-to-wear and mass market, 6-Japan

stantly searching for inspiration, which can come from almost anywhere, from comic books to animals to modern art. Courses in fashion history may give you ideas. Try to keep a sketchbook with you at all times–you never know when inspiration may strike. Your goal is to build a "signature look"–one that may eventually be part of your brand. For example, designer Diane von Furstenberg's signature wrap dress is a timeless design that people recognize as uniquely hers.

College is made for exploration, and here you may find one area of design that best suits you. You may specialize in swimwear or men's suits or skateboarding clothes or skiwear. You may focus on footwear, neckties, handbags, or jewelry. Or maybe you'll find you just enjoy making doggie socks.

Learning the business side is essential to your success. Fashion school introduces you to the costs of materials and labor. You'll get an inside look at how clothes are produced on a much larger scale. How do companies manufacture thousands of outfits–all identical but all available in different sizes? Which colors are most popular? How do you display clothes in a store so people will buy them?

Courses in psychology can prepare you to better understand why people make buying decisions. And communications classes are helpful as you sell your ideas, convince people to support your business, and work with others in producing your fashions.

As you churn out more and more samples of your work, you will build a portfolio. A portfolio usually shows photographs and sketches of your best creations. By turning the pages in your portfolio, employers can instantly see your talent and diversity.

After college, you will find that fashion is a never-ending learning experience and that you will have to keep up with current trends, technologies, and ways of doing business, such as selling apparel online.

Fashion school might be in your future, but if you want to design clothes, there's no reason not to begin right away. Just remember, learning these skills takes time and patience–don't be discouraged when you have to rip out seams and start over. Dress your friends, dress your cat, dress anyone who will stand still long enough for you to drape some fabric over them. Any experience will sharpen your skills.

FIND OUT MORE

Seek out a local store, such as a boutique, that makes and sells its own clothing designs. See if you can talk to the owner (who is often the designer) and arrange for a tour of his or her studio. Ask plenty of questions: How did you get started in fashion? What kind of training did you have? Who or what inspires you? Find out as much as you can about what this job is really like on a day-to-day basis. If you hit it off with the designer, that person might even consider mentoring you.

CHAPTER 5

Finding the Right Fit

Designers may create the styles, but bringing their vision to life requires many specialists, from the models that show the designs to those who sell the garments. In some of these fashion jobs, you may never even touch a stitch of clothing, but you'll still be playing an important role in the fashion industry. Which of these jobs is tailored just for your talents and interests?

Today's fashion models weigh 23 percent less than the average female.

Assistant Designer

A great way to learn how to be a top designer is to assist one. In this job you learn all the fundamental skills of fashion design. You make patterns and samples; you help shop for fabric; you sew together the trial-versions of garments. You are there to be the extra pair of hands for the hurried designer.

Buyer

If you love shopping for clothes and shoes, you might decide, "I should be a buyer!" If you really think about what you and your friends buy, you may actually have a talent for this job. Buyers purchase garments from the designers and manufacturers to sell in stores. They have a keen sense of fashion trends

"Clothes make the man. Naked people have little or no influence on society."

—Mark Twain

Any magazine editor will tell you that their success is in paying attention to the details.

and purchasing habits. They carefully order to meet demand and keep the garment racks stocked. They're good at tracking sales, sticking to budgets, and following what sells in the fashion world. If you can get a part-time job in high school selling clothes, you'll better understand what people are buying–and that's key to the job.

NAME: Sara Lamm
OFFICIAL TITLE: Model

What do you do?

I model clothes mostly for print advertising. I've worked for J. Crew, Brooks Brothers, Kate Spade, and Laura Ashley. It's exciting to see the clothes for next season. And it's a great job if you like to travel. I've been to a lot of places and stayed in a lot of nice hotels. Almost every day you're working with a new group of people, so you have to know how to get along with others. As a model, you learn what it's like to have business relationships with people and how to be professional.

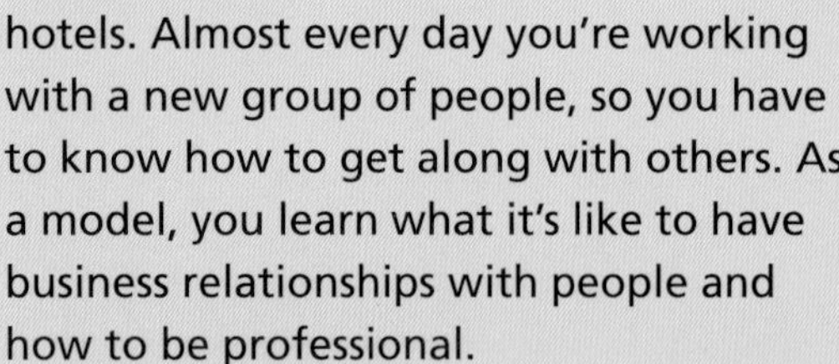

It's not all glamour. The days can be long. They often start at about 7 a.m. You have to show up with clean hair and no makeup so a makeup artist and hair stylist can get you ready. You may wear 14 or 15 outfits during the day. A busy day is 16 or 17 shots. If you shoot on location, you may have to change behind a tree, or you may be in high heels, but you have to stand on a hillside. You definitely need stamina. And you can't be afraid to have people touching you—all day long people are touching your face, your hair; your clothes—zipping up your pants, fidgeting with your belt, or rolling up your cuffs. Because the most important thing being photographed is not *you*, it's the clothes.

You have to feel comfortable in front of the camera. You have to listen and understand the idea behind the photograph. If you're modeling clothes to wear while sailing, you want to be able to translate that into smiling, laughing, and having a good time. If the clothes are more sophisticated, you might look more serious.

There's also a lot of competition and rejection. You can walk in for an audition and there might be 75 girls there for one job. For every job you get, there are 10 that you don't get. It's really important to have a sense of your own self-worth that's independent from the job.

How did you get started?

I started after college when I moved to New York. I went out to dinner with a woman by chance who was casting for a modeling job. I wound up getting the job. It was for Barneys. It was a sweet little booklet with just me, and it told the story of a couple falling in love and then breaking up. It was a high-profile project to start with. It helped me get other jobs.

Costume Designer

If you think fashion design is for you and you also have an interest in theater, you might consider costume design. These professionals create the garments worn by actors in television, film, theater, and concert productions. Often the clothes have to capture a certain time period, and designers do research to make sure the styles and fabrics they use are historically accurate. They collaborate with actors and directors to get the right looks for the players. They are usually skilled seamstresses or tailors as well as illustrators, sketching out their ideas for each scene of the show.

Fashion Editor

Elle, Teen Vogue, GQ, Marie Claire, Seventeen, W–fashion magazines crowd the shelves at grocery stores, newsstands, and gas station mini-markets. These magazines may seem like nothing but fashion advertisements, but they also feature articles on the fashion industry, trends, and popular culture. Fashion publications feature their own photo spreads and reporting. These publications wield a lot of power in the industry. Anna Wintour, the editor in chief of *Vogue* magazine, is one of the most powerful women in fashion. (The character of Miranda Priestly in the movie *The Devil Wears Prada* is based on Wintour.) Journalists in this field specialize in writing about fashion, and the editors oversee all the creative elements that go into the magazine. Many in this field have earned degrees in journalism or English, and they have a passion for all things fashion.

The Miniskirt and the Market

Some people see a connection between the length of a woman's skirt and the performance of the stock market. The "hemline effect," an economic theory devised in the 1920s, says that when hemlines go up, the market rises, and vice versa. Test this theory for yourself: The front page of most daily newspapers features a graph illustrating the stock market's performance. Over the course of a month, keep track of whether the market is, on average, up or down. (Or ask your parents—they can probably tell you!) Then surf the fashion sites to find out whether skirts are generally short or long. Is the theory right?

Fashion Illustrator

While many designers have the talent to draw their own visions, some rely on illustrators to sketch out the basic concepts. These artists may work closely with a designer in the early stages of developing a

Big Business

Fashion may be an art, but fashion design is a Business, with a capital B. Kristie Burrill, a designer in Washington, began her own fashion business at age 13 when she created a "little pink catalog" of homemade Barbie clothes that she sold for 75 cents each. To find out if you've got any business savvy, let's see how you respond to the following statements:

1 I like to help plan school fund-raisers, like bake sales and car washes. (Agree/Disagree)

2 I can't be bothered with numbers—I am an artist! (Agree/Disagree)

3 When I buy something I always check the receipt. (Agree/Disagree)

4 My parents give me a "clothing allowance," but I blew it all on candy and video games. (Agree/Disagree)

5 Math is hard, but I like to challenge myself. (Agree/Disagree)

If your answers make a nice little pattern of agree/disagree/agree/disagree/agree, then you might have the business sense to make it in the fashion biz. If numbers make you nervous, you'll have to work at getting over your fear.

clothing line, and they may also draw apparel, shoes, and accessories for ad campaigns. A lot of the work is still done by hand, but when detailed drawings are required, the illustrator may turn to CAD (computer-aided design) software. Illustrators apply their trade on the retail end as well, working with stores to design their advertisements, catalogs, and in-store displays.

Fashion Photographer

Photographers have an important role in the world of fashion. They capture the excitement of runway shows for magazines and

NAME: Brigitte Conti
OFFICIAL TITLE: Fashion Professor

What do you do?

I teach sewing and design studio, which is design of a garment from concept up to finished garment. In the sewing class, I teach all the techniques needed to create a garment, from threading a needle to using the sewing machines. Most of the big designers don't sew, but they know all the techniques.

In the sewing class, we make three garments in one semester. The final garment is [the student's] own design. In the design studio course, we take a garment from concept to finish. We start with six weeks of brainstorming. Inspiration may come from anywhere—literature, music, architecture, the spiritual world. My students learn how to combine fabric and make a texture.

I love to teach. It's very inspiring to me. I tell my students, if you see anything you like in a magazine—it could be a color, texture, ambience—then rip the page out. Keep it for inspiration.

How did you get started?

I studied a lot of chemistry, and I first worked in the perfume industry. When I married, we moved to England. I was so bored in the countryside that I started to sew some garments. When we moved to Paris, I started making jackets. I was just doing it for myself and my daughter, but my husband said you should do a business with that. When we moved to New York, I went to Parsons and studied fashion. I was 40 years old and I was completely into it. I knew it was what I had to do. After two years, I started to do my own line, selling to private shoppers. I did a lot of custom design. I was making the patterns. I was making all the samples myself.

Then when I had to produce an actual garment, I had a seamstress working for me. I registered my trademark Manouche and started to sell my designs to specialty stores in America. I did that for a few seasons—two seasons per year. Now I'm selling to 50 stores in America. I also run my own boutique called Manouche. The store allows me to test selling my products in my own store.

ON THE JOB

Then, Parsons asked me to come and teach. I tell my students, you can be very talented in design, but you really need a business background. You need a lot of investment to build the business. I needed to do a business plan. I also teach them that to succeed, you also have to be yourself. If you are just copying other people, you are not being yourself.

NAME: Kamie Chang Kahlo
OFFICIAL TITLE: Stylist/Designer

What do you do?

I've worked for 13 years as a fashion stylist, and I also run a fashion boutique that is going online (http://www.adelitastyle.com). As a stylist, I work for different photographers and for Eddie Bauer, REI, and The North Face, doing lots of snowboarding apparel. My job is to make the clothes look pretty. I may get a call that Tommy Bahama [a line of "island-inspired" clothes] needs a *flat* stylist. A flat stylist arranges clothes on a flat surface instead of on a model or mannequin. I might have to create an environment as well. For Tommy Bahama, I might put sand down or a bamboo mat to give a feel you're at the beach. Then I lay the clothes down on top of that.

I also work with models. I like to dote over the models. They put themselves out there in front of the camera, so I treat them very well. You have to be very social to be a stylist and ready for anything. Sometimes I'm working in a cubicle with no frills; other times the shoot is catered and on the beach. The hardest part is meeting new clients and proving yourself all over again. That challenges you, though, and gives you a chance to get even better at your job.

ON THE JOB

How did you get started?

I was nerdy in middle school. I didn't get fashion right away. I was more into decorating my room and getting it to look perfect. I was really good with color.

When I was 18, living in Laguna Beach, I worked at a boutique. I started doing merchandising and displaying. Merchandising and styling are closely related. In merchandising, you take a product and you make it look right to sell. If a product isn't doing well, sometimes I just move it and it does really well. You move it to the front of the store, or sometimes you do something simple—I'd take a T-shirt that is hanging and fold it. Suddenly that T-shirt would sell much better.

Eventually, I opened my own boutique called Adelita. I'm working with my mother now to design my own clothes. I'm designing these tank tops—embellishing them, adding trim and buttons. My mother is teaching me how to do it by hand. All these clothes are going to be one of a kind. My style is very whimsical. Some people think fashion is always a serious thing, but I think it's fun and lighthearted. It's the same thing you did as a little kid when you had so much fun dressing up. It's about expressing yourself and pushing your character and personality.

newspapers. They collaborate with marketers to create unique visions for their ad campaigns. They shoot models for covers and spreads in fashion magazines. Photographers rely on a keen visual sense. They know how to emphasize colors and moods in their images, and they work well with people, giving directions and drawing out expression and intensity from their models. On the technical side, they know all about cameras and lighting.

Marketer

You may be an amazing designer, but your clothes may never be popular unless you have savvy marketing. A fashion marketer knows how to get consumers interested in apparel. A marketer studies what people buy and why they buy items. They know about the hottest trends, colors, and styles. They help create the advertising campaigns and other visuals that grab consumers' attention and sell clothes. Fashion advertising is a very artistic endeavor that involves intense creativity, passion, and an understanding of the market. Marketing professionals may dream up concepts for advertising photographs and television commercials. A marketer may try to give a clothing line a boost by having a celebrity wear the designs.

Merchandiser

When you're in a department store and walk past the mannequins, signs, and arrangement of clothes on display, you're seeing the talents of the visual merchandiser. These displays can be flashy with large, colorful photographs and signs, or they may be more subtle when pushing business attire. Window dressers are merchandisers that specialize in setting up elaborate storefront windows designed to stop street traffic and lure customers in from the sidewalks. Merchandisers may sometimes act as buyers, purchasing clothing and accessories for the stores in which they work.

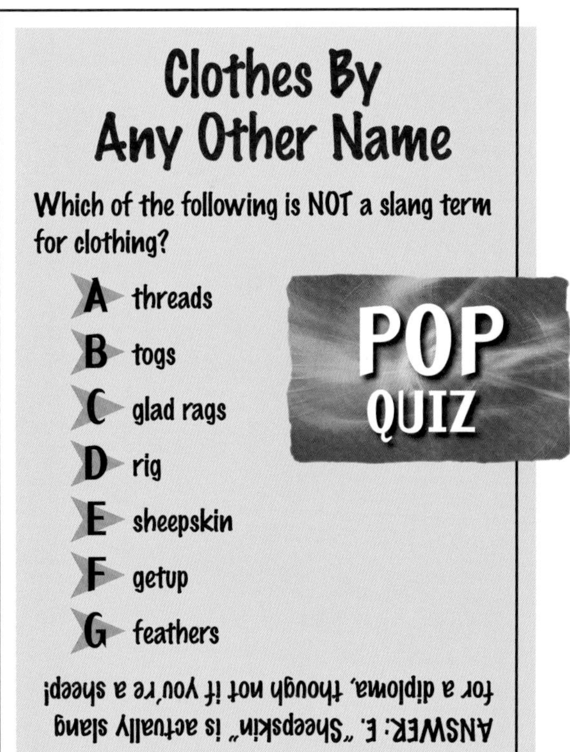

Fun Fashions

CHECK IT OUT

Fashion is a serious business, but over the years some styles have been more playful than others. You can search for images of the following goofy fashions on the Web:

- poodle skirts
- beer-can hats
- platform shoes with lucite heels featuring goldfish "swimming" inside
- paper dresses
- Campbell's Soup can pants

There's also the marketing merchandiser, who sells a fashion brand to the stores. As a marketing merchandiser, you arrange the clothes on a sales floor so they look appealing to the buyers from department stores and boutiques. You work closely with marketing, reporting on what sells and what doesn't.

A third type of merchandiser deals with product development. In this career, you dream up ideas for products for a company to make. You may think a line of embellished jeans would be perfect for American Eagle. First, you study the market and write a report on why your product will sell. Then you help with design–suggesting popular colors, sizes, and fabrics. If the company likes your samples, you will guide the new item into production and it will soon be on display in the stores.

Model

Fashion designers rely on models, fashion shoots, and runways to show their designs to their best advantage. Good models know how to walk and pose and bring the garments to life. Most modeling jobs require a certain look: very tall and slender with even features. Maintaining this look takes constant dedication to keeping fit and eating right. Some jobs for catalogs or plus-size clothing require models with a more "average" appearance. "Parts" models show just their hands (to display jewelry, for example), or their feet or legs to model footwear. Fitting models work in manufacturers' showrooms where they help designers and clothes-makers determine what's working and what isn't with an outfit. They know a lot about clothes and are there to help finalize a design.

Pattern Maker

A pattern maker can be a designer's closest and most important coworker. In this job, you work with the designer to create the "blueprint" for each piece of clothing, which indicates how the

NAME: Paul Trapani
OFFICIAL TITLE: Fashion Photographer

What do you do?

I work in San Francisco doing a lot of fashion shoots. I work at the *San Francisco Weekly*, and I've done spreads for national magazines—*The Source, InStyle, Elle Girl,* and *Planet*, a global culture magazine. It's a whirlwind doing an editorial shoot.

I've done a lot of what's called *model testing*. The models hire me to shoot a few different looks for their portfolios—head shots, beauty shots, fashion shots... The goal is to show off the model the best way possible and give them different looks.

You're not just hanging out with models, though. There's a lot of business stuff to take care of. The most difficult part for me is the business side. All I want to do is make images. There are days I come home at 11 at night. When I don't have shoots, I'm marketing. I love the freedom of working for myself, and the excitement of working for a cool magazine. This is a very dynamic job.

How did you get started?

When I was in high school, I would take pages from fashion magazines and try to mimic the shots with my sister or someone else in the photo. It didn't occur to me at first that you could make a living with photography, so I studied business at college. But when I finished, I decided I just had to go to New York and assist photographers. I assisted David LaChapelle [a famous fashion photographer], and if I saw a photographer I liked in a magazine, I would just call them up and say, do you need an assistant? I'd even do it for free to get in. I learned the bulk of what I know about photography from my time as an assistant. Eventually I got to the point where I was assisting more than shooting so I moved to San Francisco and promised myself I wouldn't go back to assisting.

My advice to young photographers is to shoot every day. Take pictures of whatever you can and develop your eye. Take pictures of your friends, your dog, the trees, the sky. I shot a roll a day for a year and it really helped me. I even took pictures of myself on the subway or my foot while I was eating a burrito. It's a great lesson.

"About half my designs are controlled fantasy, 15 percent are total madness, and the rest are bread-and-butter designs."

—SHOE DESIGNER MANOLO BLAHNIK

garment should be assembled. Patterns are the measurements and shapes of fabrics that will be cut out and sewn together into a final form. You create a master pattern that manufacturers follow to make copies of that garment. You may use computer-aided design (CAD) software to draft the patterns. Related to this career is pattern grading. Pattern graders reduce or enlarge a pattern so the manufacturer can make a range of sizes, from petite to extra-large. Graders also use computer programs to help them calculate these measurements.

Personal Stylist

Sometimes called wardrobe consultants and personal shoppers, stylists work closely with individuals to help them look their best. They take a close look at a client's physical features and lifestyle and then come up with fashion choices that will help the person achieve his or her desired look. Stylists may teach classes on the subject. Some work exclusively with celebrities, who depend on always looking their best.

Retailer

The motto of the retailer should be sell, sell, sell! Retailers sell clothing directly to the public. They might be the managers of major department stores or boutique owners. They often wear many hats, planning which designs to sell, taking care of hiring and firing, and handling all financial aspects of the business. Their success depends on sales, so they often talk to their customers to find out what they want. Retailers also decide how much inventory (items on the shelves and in the storeroom) to have in the store.

Seamstress or Tailor

If you want to really be on the cutting edge of fashion, you should become a seamstress or tailor. These skilled people work hands-on in constructing clothes–using scissors and sewing by hand and machine. They need to be nimble-fingered and precise–taking measurements of models and making adjustments so the clothes fit perfectly. They work closely with pattern makers or they're sometimes pattern makers themselves. Their practical talents are essential to the craft, and many famous fashion designers first honed their skills as seamstresses and tailors.

Trend Spotter

Want a job in fashion where you predict the future? Trend spotting is just that. You have to predict what will be popular next season. Trend spotters work in the marketing area, and they are in touch with what's "hot"–they watch hit TV shows, read lots of magazines, and visit malls to see what young people are buying. Trend spotters work for major clothing manufacturers and stores and help them decide which garments to produce.

FUN FACTOID

Talk about big business! More people are busy buying, selling, and producing clothing than any other industry in the world.

CHAPTER 6

Kids Ask, Fashion Designers Answer

To find out what kids really wanted to know about this profession, we went to the source and asked real middle school students for questions they would ask a working fashion designer. We posed their questions to two busy young designers–Alison Dahl Kelly and Sean Shin.

Alison Kelly received national attention when she appeared on Season Three of *Project Runway* on Bravo TV. She studied fine arts and metalsmithing in Mexico, and she incorporates her own sterling silver clasps and notions into many of her garments. Her first line, Run R1ot, soon became Dahl, a line of one-of-a-kind dresses, tops, and jackets popular with celebrities such as Hillary Duff. (You can see Alison's designs at http://www.atelierdahl.com.)

Giselle Bündchen held the title of highest-paid model in 2006, earning more than $15 million a year. (Source: Forbes)

Sean Shin specializes in menswear. He is currently an assistant designer in the menswear department at Geoffrey Beene. Beene was known for his simple, comfortable, and dressy designs for women, but he also made clothes for men. He died in 2004, but his popular brand lives on. Sean and four other classmates from FIT also designed men's outfits for the band Panic! at the Disco. Sean plans on introducing his own line of men's fashion in the near future.

"Ideas come from the world around us."

—Alison Kelly, Fashion Designer

How did you get started in fashion?

–Shannon M., age 11

Alison: My mother taught me to sew at a very young age. She made all of my dresses for special occasions, Halloween costumes, even matching dresses for my dolls. Being creative and designing clothing ourselves became a sacred process for me, one that can be repeated over and over again, bringing with it inspiration and satisfying self-expression. [Alison has been making her own clothing since she was 14 years old.]

Natalie C.

Sean: I had studied industrial design, but I felt that there was something missing from my life. I felt that my real identity was in fashion, so I applied to the Fashion Institute of Technology. I was the first Korean scholar in their menswear department. I took courses in pattern making by hand and computer, knitting, construction, and fashion drawing, among others. It wasn't easy to learn about fashion design for two years, but I always told myself, "Just go for it, Sean!"

How do you come up with your ideas?

–Natalie C., age 11

Alison: Ideas come from the world around us. It can be as simple as watching a bird frolicking around or as complex as quantum mechanics. What intrigues me the most are patterns

Sean Shin

you find in nature–the way a flower blossoms or the intricate designs you see on seashells and rocks. I guess my inspiration is more organic. I am completely driven by music–listening to music, playing music, singing. I find music to be my life force.

Sean: Every day, I get inspiration everywhere I go–at museums, shopping, reading fashion magazines. I always bring my camera to capture that inspiration. I also sketch my ideas for new designs. This is the best way to keep recording my inspirations.

Do you base your ideas on clothes you like to wear?

–Megan R., age 11

Alison: I only wear my own designs, except for footwear, where I mostly wear handcrafted CYDWOQ brand. I wear

"Every day, I get inspiration everywhere I go–at museums, shopping, reading fashion magazines."

—SEAN SHIN, FASHION DESIGNER

outfits that suit my mood, and my designs come from intuitive reasoning and surface inspiration, like fabrics or patterns. I am always designing with myself in mind, as I feel I must fully respect my work and feel proud wearing it. I keep my older, more conservative sister in mind when I design, as well as my mother and friends with different body shapes. I want everyone to be able to wear my designs and feel confident in their own skin.

Sean: Nope! I wish I could, but for some reason, I've been making all of my garments for skinny, tall men. I'm kind of short at five foot eight inches. I actually wear plain styles such as solid, black, long-sleeved T-shirts with gray cardigans and black denim pants and sneakers. In my design, though, I am always concerned about the runway show. If people see my garments, I want them to feel excited by my clothes. My stuff is always based on a simple outfit and color, but there is something special in the details or eccentric shapes.

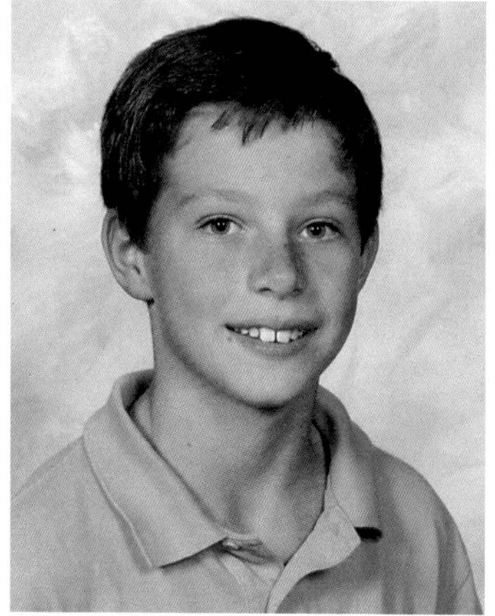

Mitchell C.

What is your average day like? Do you have an office or do you work from home?

–Mitchell C., age 11

Alison: I do most of my computer work and initial design processes at home. I use an industrial sewing machine and a special serger sewing machine. I make the first samples on myself. I have a professional pattern maker and seamstress in the garment district in Manhattan where I'll go a few times a week. I go over samples with them as well.

Sean: I assist in the design process for knits and sweaters at the offices of Geoffrey Beene. I attend meetings and share my ideas with the design team. It's sometimes really tough to keep up with all the work, but when I see the customer who buys our products in the store, it makes me feel proud doing this job. I am really learning the design process from start to finish.

What is your favorite part of the job?

–Erin M., age 11

Alison: My favorite part of being a designer is when I'll be wearing a dress, for instance, and someone will be inspired by it. My goal is to make people happy and inspired, and if that is accomplished every once in a while, then I feel I am doing something toward the greater good of this world.

Sean: Learning a new design process! I now assist in the design of knits and sweaters, which I hadn't done before, so it is exciting to do this work. I'm pretty sure it's going to be really helpful for my future career in fashion.

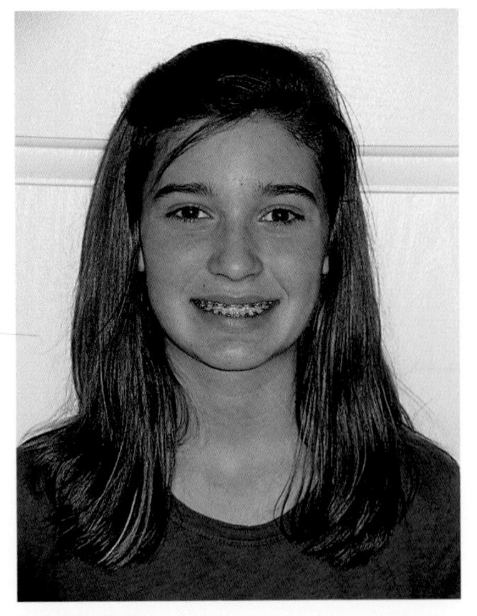
Megan R.

How do you decide what colors are "in"?

–Megan R., age 11

Alison: I find it to be intuitive. Some design houses will pay thousands and thousands of dollars for "trend research." I feel it in my bones. I always see the more progressive designers coming out with very similar trends, color schemes, cuts, fabric choices–it amazes me. Sometimes we just all "know" what we want–the colors we want to see and touch.

Sean: I always get my colors from the concept, so it's pretty flexible. If I want to go for a crazy theme, I pick bright colors. But I do have my favorite colors, which are brown and gray, so I always try to put them into my new designs.

Alison Kelly

When you design clothes do you think about what is fashionable or what will sell? What types of clothes do you like designing best?

–Templeton K., age 10

Alison: I aim to design collections that will accommodate many different body types, and be aesthetically pleasing and interesting. Dresses are my favorite article of clothing to make, next comes jackets, then more simple things like T-shirts and sweatshirts for boys.

Sean: I always picture the specific person who would like to wear my clothes before I design. To me, the design I like best comes from how much I understand the person who is interested in my fashion.

I like sports. What sports would be great for showing off cool fashion?

–Templeton K., age 10

Alison: Any. The trend has already begun. Look how innovative female tennis stars' outfits and basketball jerseys have become. Stella McCartney for Adidas, for example.

Sean: There are lots of places for fashion in sports. In my opinion, I would say, baseball and basketball. I know those sports have already been showing off cool fashion, but for me, it's getting boring to see the same styles every year.

CHAPTER 7

Virtual Apprentice

FASHION DESIGNER FOR A DAY

Wondering whether you've got the eye for beauty and the head for business that it takes to succeed in this field? Here's a timeline of activities to help you try this career on for size. You can work independently or team up with other students to turn your classroom into a design studio.

8:00 Get up and get moving! There's not a minute to waste in this field. Begin by brainstorming ideas (on your own or in teams) for a design collection. Sources of inspiration can come from anywhere—from colors, shapes, historical events, songs, words, images, and even objects. (An entire collection inspired by kitchen gadgets? Why not!) Take notes and gather anything tangible (samples of fabric, postcards, dried leaves) together in a paper bag.

9:00 Assemble a "mood board" (that is, a collage) using fabric swatches and images from fashion magazines. Include images, color samples, bits of text, pieces of fabric, and whatever else you find to express your fashion ideas. Designers often use mood boards to communicate their ideas and concepts to other members of the design team.

10:00 Some designers develop their design ideas by draping fabric on a dressmaker's dummy and watching how the material falls around the human form. Team up with a friend or classmate and practice your draping skills. You'll need a bed sheet, a sash or belt, and some large safety pins. Take turns draping the sheet around each other and belting or pinning the material in various ways. Start with a classic toga look and see how many different styles you can come up with. Be sure to have your model walk so you can see how your design behaves on a moving figure.

11:00 Create three different design sketches, using your mood board for inspiration. If you're not a skilled artist, you can trace over human figures in magazines and then add clothing shapes on top of these forms. If you're working with other students, you can team up on this assignment. One person can draw and the others can contribute ideas.

12:00 Grab some lunch on the run. You'll need plenty of protein to fuel you through a fashion designer's busy day.

1:00 Accessorize it! If you're working on this project with your class, have everyone bring in at least three different accessories (belts, hats, scarves, costume jewelry, handbags, and footwear). Put these in a common pile that everyone can draw from. Work together to choose accessories that best complement your designs. If you're working independently, just raid your own closet (or your mom's or dad's) for accessories that would enhance the looks you've created.

2:00 Put together a fashion portfolio to showcase your designs. Decorate the outside of a folder with a trademark that you create for yourself or your design team. Include in the folder your mood board, the sketches you've drawn, and a list or sketches of the accessories you chose to enhance your looks.

3:00 The moment of truth has arrived: Time to present your collection to a friend, parent, or your classmates. Talk them through your design concepts, show them your sketches, and—finally—ask for their (honest) feedback on your creations.

4:00 Good designers know that clothes don't sell themselves. Write a one-page ad concept for the clothing you've designed. Think about the type of person you imagine would want to buy your clothing designs. What setting, type of music, and language would most appeal to them?

5:00 Take a look at what you're wearing. Does it reflect your unique style? If your clothes don't say "Future Fashion Designer," it's time to rethink your fashion choices. Go through your wardrobe and come up with some interesting new ways to mix up what you've got.

Virtual Apprentice

FASHION DESIGNER: FIELD REPORT

If this is your book, use the space below to jot down a few notes about your Virtual Apprentice experience (or use a blank sheet of paper if this book doesn't belong to you). What did you do? What did you learn? Which activities did you enjoy the most? Don't be stingy with the details.

8:00 INSPIRATION!: ____________________

9:00 MOOD BOARD: ____________________

10:00 DRAPING: ____________________

11:00 DESIGN SKETCHES: ____________________

12:00 LUNCH:

1:00 ACCESSORIZING:

2:00 FASHION PORTFOLIO:

3:00 DESIGN PRESENTATION:

4:00 AD CONCEPT:

5:00 PERSONAL STYLE ASSESSMENT:

Count Me In (or Out)

FUTURE FASHIONISTA?

Were you the kid who was too busy making amazing outfits for your dolls or dressing your dog in the latest canine fashions to bother with playing video games or shooting baskets? You never miss an episode of *Project Runway*, but you're still not sure whether you're cut out to be a professional fashion designer. Read the following questions and record your answers on a separate piece of paper. Before you enroll in fashion design school, check back to see whether this profession is a good fit for you.

Quick, what's your style? Retro or sporty? Goth or classic? Hip-hop, boho, grunge, or some really inspired mix of all of the above? What you wear speaks volumes about the kind of person you are. On a separate piece of paper, write down the story that your clothes are telling about YOU. (If you have a hard time answering this question, your own personal style is probably still evolving, or you may not care enough about fashion to be aware of what your clothes communicate about you.)

What are your favorite styles of the past? Which styles do you hope never come back into fashion?

____

____

____

____

What is your vision of the future of fashion? What do you imagine people will be wearing 100 years from today?

____

____

____

Do you think fashion is important? Why or why not? (Would all the money people spend on clothes be better invested somewhere else?)

____

____

____

Complete these sentences with the first word, phrase, or name that comes to mind.

1. The article of clothing I have had the longest is my ____________________.

I still have it because ______________________________.

2. My favorite fashion designer is ______________________________.

I like her/his designs because they are ______________________________

and ______________________________________.

3. The style icon I most admire is ______________________________

because ______________________________________.

4. If money was no object, I would wear ______________________________

5. To work in the fashion world, I need to learn ______________________________

____.

When I am invited to a formal or "black-tie" event, most of my energy goes toward:

a. Trying to think up a good excuse to worm out of it.

b. Choosing the perfect outfit to wear.

c. Getting up the nerve to ask someone to come with me.

d. Browsing fabric stores for inspiration for the original outfit I plan to make and wear.

e. Mowing all the lawns in the neighborhood to earn enough cash to buy a stylish pair of shoes.

(If you answered d, you are well on your way to developing the flair for fashion all successful designers share.)

More Resources for Young Fashion Designers

BOOKS

Gehlhar, Mary. *The Fashion Designer Survival Guide*. Chicago: Kaplan Business, 2005.

Jones, Jen. *Fashion Careers: Finding the Right Fit*. Minneapolis: Capstone Press, 2007.

Jones, Jen. *Fashion Design: The Art of Style*. Minneapolis: Capstone Press, 2007.

Jones, Jen. *Fashion Design School: Learning the Skills to Succeed*. Minneapolis: Capstone Press, 2007

Jones, Jen. *Fashion History: Looking Great Through the Ages.* Minneapolis: Capstone Press, 2007.

Jones, Jen. *Fashion Trends: How Popular Style Is Shaped.*Minneapolis: Capstone Press, 2007.

Maze, Stephanie. *I Want to Be a Fashion Designer*. San Diego, Calif.: Harcourt Paperbacks, 2000.

PROFESSIONAL ASSOCIATIONS

Council of Fashion Designers of America
1412 Broadway, Suite 2006
New York, New York 10018
http://www.cfda.com

International Association of Clothing Designers and Executives
835 Northwest 36th Terrace
Oklahoma City, Oklahoma 73118
http://www.iacde.com

WEB SITES

The Internet and fashion are a match made in heaven. A gazillion great sites let you browse through the fashions of yesterday and today, and individual designers' collections can be viewed as slide shows that give you a front row seat (move over, Anna Wintour!) under the fashion tents. Here are few sites we really like:

The Costume Institute at the Metropolitan Museum of Art (see the Collection Highlights, especially the dress by Ji Eon Kang made entirely out of metal museum tags!)
http:www.metmuseum.org/Works_of_Art/department
.asp?dep=8

Design a virtual fashion collection and send it down a cyber-runway! This site features links to lots of virtual fashion show games
http://www.dressupgames.com/fashion.html

Also chock full of fascinating info is the Fashion Era Web site
http://www.fashion-era.com

The Museum of Costume in Bath, England
http://www.museumofcostume.co.uk

The Victoria and Albert Museum in London has a great site
http://www.vam.ac.uk